MW00646977

SURRENDER AND FREEDOM

SWAMI DAYANANDA SARASWATI

ARSHA VIDYA

ARSHA VIDYA
RESEARCH AND PUBLICATION TRUST
CHENNAI

Published by :
Arsha Vidya Research
and Publication Trust
32 / 4 ' Sri Nidhi ' Apts III Floor
Sir Desika Road Mylapore
Chennai 600 004 INDIA
Tel   : 044 2499 7023
Telefax: 2499 7131
Email : avrandpc@gmail.com

ISBN : 978 - 81 - 904203 - 5- 8

Revised Edition : August 2007   Copies : 2000
1st Reprint   : May   2009   Copies : 2000

Design :
Suchi Ebrahim

Printed by :
Sudarsan Graphics
27, Neelakanta Mehta Street
T. Nagar, Chennai 600 017
Email : info@sudarsan.com

CONTENTS

v

KEY TO TRANSLITERATION AND PRONUNCIATION OF
SANSKRIT LETTERS

Sanskrit is a highly phonetic language and hence accuracy in articulation of the letters is important. For those unfamiliar with the *Devanāgari* script, the international transliteration is a guide to the proper pronunciation of Sanskrit letters.

अ	a	(but)		ट	ṭa	(true)*3
आ	ā	(father)		ठ	ṭha	(anthill)*3
इ	i	(it)		ड	ḍa	(drum)*3
ई	ī	(beat)		ढ	ḍha	(godhead)*3
उ	u	(full)		ण	ṇa	(under)*3
ऊ	ū	(pool)		त	ta	(path)*4
ऋ	ṛ	(rhythm)		थ	tha	(thunder)*4
ॠ	ṝ	(marine)		द	da	(that)*4
ऌ	ḷ	(revelry)		ध	dha	(breathe)*4
ए	e	(play)		न	na	(nut)*4
ऐ	ai	(aisle)		प	pa	(put) 5
ओ	o	(go)		फ	pha	(loophole)*5
औ	au	(loud)		ब	ba	(bin) 5
क	ka	(seek) 1		भ	bha	(abhor)*5
ख	kha	(blockhead)*1		म	ma	(much) 5
ग	ga	(get) 1		य	ya	(loyal)
घ	gha	(log hut)*1		र	ra	(red)
ङ	ṅa	(sing) 1		ल	la	(luck)
च	ca	(chunk) 2		व	va	(vase)
छ	cha	(catch him)*2		श	śa	(sure)
ज	ja	(jump) 2		ष	ṣa	(shun)
झ	jha	(hedgehog)*2		स	sa	(so)
ञ	ña	(bunch) 2		ह	ha	(hum)

•	ṁ	anusvāra	(nasalisation of preceding vowel)
:	ḥ	visarga	(aspiration of preceding vowel)
*			No exact English equivalents for these letters

1.	Guttural	–	Pronounced from throat
2.	Palatal	–	Pronounced from palate
3.	Lingual	–	Pronounced from cerebrum
4.	Dental	–	Pronounced from teeth
5.	Labial	–	Pronounced from lips

The 5th letter of each of the above class – called nasals – are also pronounced nasally.

Every tradition, secular or religious, has a concept of surrender, whether it is from this country or elsewhere. There is also a promised end that comes with this surrender. Even secular traditions want you to surrender your ideologies, your concepts, to their ideologies and concepts. Even Mao, who denounced all religions, wanted you to surrender to his 'Red Book'. And he promised certain success in life. Thus, I find that both the secular and the religious people want you to surrender.

In addition to these traditions, there are also rationalists, who, though small in number, consider themselves as 'thinking people'. They say, "Do not surrender, because the most selfish is the most happy." They even quote the *upaniṣad*[1] to support their view, *"ātmanastu kāmāya sarvaṁ priyaṁ bhavati,* everything is dear to you for the sake of the self alone." Of course, that is a misinterpretation because this statement of the *upaniṣad* does not mean that you have to be selfish to be happy.

---

[1] *Bṛhadāraṇyakopaniṣad 4.5.6*

SURRENDER CAN BE EXPLOITED

When someone wants you to surrender to him or her, it is generally for his or her own self-image. Even though, in one's own opinion about oneself, one does not value himself or herself as somebody, one wants people to look up to him or her. When a few people look up to the person, one feels, "I am looked up to and so I must be somebody." But then, if one is very sure, "I am somebody," one will not require others to surrender, or to look up to one.

In surrender, there is always the possibility of exploitation. When you surrender to somebody, that somebody can exploit you to any extent. This has been the problem of the *guru-śiṣya-paramparā*. The *guru* is considered to be the ultimate altar of surrender. They say *śive ruṣṭe gurustrātā*, when Lord Śiva is angry, *guru* will protect you from that anger. *Gurau ruṣṭe ko'pi na trātā*, but when the *guru* is angry, no Lord cannot protect you. Therefore, do everything to please the *guru*; do not make the *guru* angry.

Why should the *guru* get angry? I thought a *guru* is supposed to make me free from anger. If the *guru* himself gets angry, what kind of *guru* is he? What is he going to teach me? How is he going to help me? It is unfortunate that some people think anger is necessary to get things done. They get angry if things do not go their way. Such people have weaknesses and are easily exploited by people around them. Children, for instance, know their parents' weaknesses and learn to get things done without getting them angry. Some people want praise; others figure that out and praise them to the skies. In fact, you can get the angry people easily accede to your requests if you frame your questions properly.

There were two Zen monks. One of them went to the abbot, the chief of the monastery, and asked, "Sir, can I smoke when I walk and meditate?" The abbot said, "No." The monk told another monk, "We are not supposed to smoke when we are walking and meditating." The other monk said, "You do not know how to ask. Now see how I get the right answer." The second monk went to the abbot and asked, "Sir, can I meditate when I smoke and walk?" The abbot said, Yes"! This is how bosses get manipulated!

I know a person who could get the answer 'yes' or 'no' the way he wanted. All one has to do is to frame the question properly. There is a lot of manipulation going on in the world; people take advantage of others' weaknesses. Thus, when a *guru* gets angry, unwittingly he subjects himself to manipulation. So, wherever there is surrender, it can be exploited. It all depends upon whom I surrender to; for which we have to understand first what exactly is meant by surrender and what is freedom.

You can surrender what you own

When we say we surrender, what is it that we can surrender? We can surrender our titles, our property, money, and whatever belongings we have. We can surrender whatever we possess, but we cannot surrender our wife, our children, or our parents because we do not own any one of them. People think they can surrender their children to others. We can surrender our children when they are young, because unfortunately they cannot be consulted at that age. If we do not consult them, then it is not surrender; it is a criminal abuse.

You have no authority to surrender your children to someone else. The one who receives and the one who hands them over, both are making a mistake, because children somehow know, even if they are infants that they are not with their parents. They feel abandoned and suffer life-long pain and anger. Therefore, you have no right to surrender even your own children. You can surrender only what you own, and not what you do not. That is why I do not accept this idea of *kanyā-dāna*, giving away the daughter as a gift in marriage when she is very young. Who are you to give her away? She is her own person. Child marriage was instituted in this country because of certain historical and social problems. Married girls were left untouched by the invading armies and therefore child marriage was instituted. In child marriage, it is the parents who decide. Even though the system of child marriage is no longer in practice, the concept of giving away the daughter as gift continues in our patriarchal system. This is not the Hindu marriage that our *ṛṣis* visualised. The Hindu marriage is always a marriage for emotional maturity and it is not that someone is just given away. One partner is not less than the other. Both are equal.

The Hindu marriage is not complete unless the *sapta-padi* is performed. *Sapta-padi* is the seven steps taken by the couple together. This person is a pilgrim in progress of his journey, and she joins him; this is solemnised in marriage; the pilgrimage is undertaken together. For this pilgrimage death is not the goal, because that is the one place you do not want to go. That is an end, which will take place naturally.. But the pilgrimage is only for your own maturity.

6 SURRENDER AND FREEDOM

The seven steps are symbolic. The seventh step is for friendship; friendship is always amongst equals. There is no *dāna* involved in marriage in the sense of gifting away. You can surrender only things you own, things that have no will.

TO LIVE IS TO GROW

When we observe the creation, we find that when an organism is born it is not adequately mature. For example, when a calf is born it is not ready to live its life fully as a cow. A calf is born with a physical body, a baby body and it is born to live, not to die. To live a cow's life, however, the calf has to grow into a cow. Once the calf survives and becomes an adult, there is a real accomplishment of life for that animal. It has become an adult cow; it does not require to do anything more to become a mature cow.

A human being also is born as a baby. However, one does not even begin one's life until one becomes an adult, physically and biologically. The physical body has to grow to become an adult for which one need not do anything special; nature takes care of it. You just keep living, eating, and make sure that every time you go out, you return in one piece. In course of time, you will become an adult. This is the inbuilt nature of the body. You become a potential father or mother. You become an adult physically. It does not mean, however, that you have become an adult emotionally. Emotionally, one can still be, in fact, one is often a child.

You have come through a childhood, gathering various notions about yourself. They form your core personality. You must acknowledge this. This core personality has two-fold notions, one about yourself, and the other about the world. As a child, the world was always frightening because it was a very powerful world, something too big for a small child with no information to handle it. So, the child starts with a fear of this world. Every bug, every cockroach is a fright for the child. There are lots of people who have many phobias, many problems, picked up when they were young. The world is too vast and the child's power and knowledge are too little. Therefore, the child concludes, 'the world is out to get me'. That is why good parental care will give the child a sense of well being so that it will not have that extra fear which makes the person abnormal. Since the world is too much, one concludes, 'I am no good'. Thus, 'I am no good'or 'I am insignificant' and 'the world is too much,'are the two-fold conclusions that form the core personality of every human being.

A cow does not have these problems because it is not a self-conscious being. Its consciousness is limited only to keep its species going. A cow will recognise another cow, even though it looks entirely different. A dog will recognise another dog. Even a Great Dane will not mistake a Poodle for a cat. Thus, an animal also has self-identity, but only to the extent that it can have its species propagated; nothing more than that. If their behaviour indicates anything, I find that animals are free from all forms of complex.

SUBJECTIVE PERCEPTION

Human beings, however, are different from animals. As a human being I grow with complexes. There is no way of bringing up a child without complexes. To say, 'you should grow without complexes,' will only create yet another complex. Every human being has core opinions about the world as well as about oneself, both of which are wrong. I could not even figure out whether my parents loved me or not. When I wanted candy and my mom said, "No", I thought she did not like me. When my father and mother were quarrelling, I thought it was because of me. Thus, for want of knowledge I came to conclusions about myself, which were both silly and wrong. I made similar conclusions about the world. These conclusions form the core of every human being. The core personality gathers further problems to form a nucleus. Further disappointments and fears are gathered because every perception is completely conditioned by the core personality. Consequently one continues to be a child, emotionally.

One does not look at the world as it is. There are two worlds: one that is available for public gaze, and the other that is created by one's own imaginations, one's own perceptions. It is the world that belongs to a given person. This subjective world is called *adhyāsa*, superimposition. To see a flower as a flower is knowledge. However, if one takes a paper rose, or a plastic rose, as a real rose, it is *adhyāsa*.

When I look at the world, do I look at the world as it is or do I look at a world that I have created out of my own imaginations, set by my own mind, my own limitations, fears, anxieties, insecurities? I always look at the world from my own fears, anxieties, from my own projections. A man who does not have money thinks he is poor. That he has no money is a fact, but that he is poor is a conclusion. I have some money to burn is a fact, but 'I am rich' is a conclusion. Therefore, when I look upon myself as a poor man, and then when I see somebody going in a car, I think that that person is successful. This problem is called *adhyāsa*, superimposition. From my standpoint of feeling that I am poor, I look at the people not as they are, but look at them with my eyes of jealousy, my eyes of admiration. I look up to them; as though they are the ones that have made it; that I am nobody. Thus, each one looks at the world not as it is, but from his or her own opinion.

I look at the world with my own goggles, which have their own colour. I am not living in the public world, a world so vast and varied that gives accommodation to everyone. It is vast enough for all of us. We can live happily in it, but we do not feel it is vast enough because we see a world of our own perception. Everybody perceives the world in his or her own personal way.

Śobhanādhyāsa is seeing more than what is

You look for security all the time. You seek security in property, relation, money, and in hundred different things. All these are of some help inasmuch as they give some security. There are people who say,

'Money does not give you security. It does not do anything.' This is silly. Money does give you a sense of security, some pleasure, because you feel you have achieved something. It can provide opportunities for you to enjoy. However, if you think that money is security, then you are wrong. This kind of error is called *śobhanādhyāsa*, seeing something more than what is there. Similarly, music will give you some pleasure. It can transport you to a realm where the usual concerns are not there. For the time being, you forget your day-to-day problems, your opinions about yourself and the world. The melody in the music makes you forget these things. Therefore, music does give you pleasure, but if you think music will solve all your problems, it is not true; it is *śobhanādhyāsa*.

Similarly, if I believe that I need to be married for my life to be perfect, it is another instance of *śobhanādhyāsa*. Marriage will bring certain things in its wake, but if I do not grow in the marriage, then it can bring a few problems. So, if I see a more value in something than what it has, it is *śobhanādhyāsa*. Gold is a metal like copper or iron. As metal it is not different from any other metal. There are people who are committed to gold, while others are afraid of gold.

There is a story told about a master by his disciple. The master used to say, *kāñcana*, gold is something to be kept away. One disciple, wanted to test the master's *vairāgya*, dispassion. He placed a gold coin under the master's pillow without his knowledge. When the master went to bed, he could not sleep due to the presence of the gold coin. So great was his *vairāgya*! The disciple, who was watching all this, realised his mistake. Prostrating before the master, he admitted what he had done. The gold coin removed, the master fell asleep!

When I heard this story, a question arose in my mind as to whether the story praises the master or belittles him. Suppose, the coin belonged to someone for whom gold was everything, and he had kept the gold coin under his own pillow. He found the coin was missing when he checked before he went to sleep. Now he was not able to sleep. Here, we have a person who loses sleep because of the absence of gold coin. There is another person who is equally disturbed because of its presence. Who is the greater person? Since both of them are disturbed by gold, how can it be said that one is greater than the other?

In the master's room there might have been variety of things—a copper vessel, a steel plate, iron nails to hold his cot together, brass door knobs and locks—all of which are metal. The iron and copper do not affect the person whereas the gold does. What does it mean? Does the problem belong to the gold or to the person? The gold itself does not do anything; it just is what it is, a metal with its own objective value, like any other metal. It is Bhagavān's creation. Therefore to a God-inspired person how can gold be different from copper or iron, which is also Bhagavān's creation? Giving the benefit of doubt to the master, sometimes the praise actually diminishes the master's greatness, even though the disciples did not mean to do so.

The difference between iron and gold is an objective difference. Gold has a particular atomic weight. It is rare, highly malleable, shining metal, not subject to corrosion. These natural qualities of gold made it a valuable metal, even before it was made the basis for the monetary system. Fear of gold is a problem, an *adhyāsa*. Lord Kṛṣṇa says in the *Bhagavad Gītā*[2] "The one because of whom people do not get disturbed and who does not get disturbed by people... is dear to me." To look upon gold, therefore, as a source of bondage, is *śobhanādhyāsa*, seeing something more than what gold has got.

---

[2] *yasmānnodvijate loko lokānnodvijate ca yaḥ ... me priyaḥ* (12.15)

When we interact with people also, we do not see people as they are. First, we label them and then interact. Rarely do we meet people as they are. We meet people the way we think they are, what they are from our own perception. This means that we are stuck with ourselves, with our own projections, labels. We live, therefore, in an imagined world. This is *adhyāsa*.

We look at the world as either mine or this is how people are or this is how the world is or this is what I am. Thus, my own fears, anxieties, apprehensions, distress form the basis for a world I project. There is a world and there is a projection. These projections come from my psychological background, which is real. That background stifles my perception, my estimation of the world, and therefore I live in a world of my own projections. Unless I remove the projections I do not live in a world that is available for public perception. If I live in the public world, the set-up in which I find myself, then whatever problems, challenges I face are real, and I can meet them. But I live in a private world of my own, and the problems that I see are all my creation. Consequently, I need education with reference to my value structure. Education is to help a person surrender his or her own projections. I should first surrender my *adhyāsa*, superimposition. My superimposition of security and various other things and values upon situations, upon things, upon people is false. The immediate surrender is renunciation of my own prejudices that form the basis of my perception.

In that surrender, is there freedom or not? In that surrender alone, there is freedom, understanding, love, compassion, sympathy, sharing and friendship. Without that surrender, you are bound by your own prejudices, your own notions about the world, about yourself; there is no freedom.

LIVING IS THE GOAL OF LIFE

I am a conscious being who has come to this world to live, not to die. Death is there but it can never be the goal of my life. If death is the goal of life, why I should be born at all? I do not remain in this form after death and I was not there before birth in this form. Why should I be born to be what I was before I was born? Death, obviously, cannot be the goal of my life.

You cannot say that heaven is the goal of my life either, for I need not be born here to go to heaven. The detour makes no sense. It is like coming to Baroda from Mumbai via Pune. If I have to come to Baroda

from Mumbai, I should travel directly to Baroda.[3]
If I have to go to heaven I should go directly to heaven.
I need not come to this world. I am born here, because
I am meant to be here. The reason for my being here is
living, and not dying. Therefore, heaven cannot be the
goal of my life here. If living is the goal of life, any
goal except living is a projection, *adhyāsa*. To see this
adhyāsa as such is *viveka*, knowledge. It is also
surrender, surrender of *adhyāsa*.

In reality, I do not own anything that belongs to
me. The reason is that when I came to this world,
I was given this physical body, with an inbuilt capacity
to grow, to become an adult. It was also endowed
with a mind, and a set of senses. Thus, this body-mind-
sense-complex is given, not created by me. I consider
that what is not authored by me does not belong to
me. This body is not my creation; it does not belong
to me. If this body, which I consider my own, does
not belong to me, what else can I call my own?
Therefore, ownership is but a projection caused by
the coloured glasses of my ignorance and wrong
thinking. When I give up these glasses in the wake of

---

[3] These talks were given in Baroda, a city about 250 miles north of
Mumbai, while Pune is about 100 miles south of Mumbai.

discriminative knowledge, there is reality in my life. There is living; anything I do is real. When I say I love somebody, I mean it. When I thank somebody, I mean it, because then I no longer see the world from my subjective background; I really see the world as it is. Therefore, there is no other surrender except that of my projections, for I own hardly anything else to surrender.

OWNERSHIP IS A NOTION

Of all the projections, the most stifling is the sense of ownership. If you analyse, many of your problems come from the sense of ownership. Even though you live in a house, you are not satisfied. You live in a good house, and still pay the old rent. But that is not enough. You want to own the house. The sense of ownership seems to be a very important thing for a person to feel secure. Our *śāstra* denounces this ownership as a sham or pretence. In the first verse of *Īśāvāsyopaniṣad*, a question is asked, "*kasyasvid dhanam*, whose is the wealth?" Look upon the whole world as *Īśvara—īśā vāsyam idaṁ sarvam*.

To see how notional is ownership, consider this situation. A friend of yours, who owns a nice house with a large compound, decides to go to the United States. He asks you to 'house sit' for him while he is away. He will not charge you rent, but you are expected to pay the taxes and take care of the maintenance of the house while you live there. This is a very good deal for such a fine house and you accept the offer. Your friend, who does very well in the States, does not come back for years to claim his property.

One day while you are at work you receive an overseas telephone call from your friend to say that he gifts this house to you and has already instructed his lawyer to prepare a gift deed. That evening when you go home, even though you go to the same house, your attitude towards the house has changed. Your notion now is, "This is my house." As a person also, you are not the same; you are the owner of the house. You call a real estate broker to see how much the house is worth. You decide to put up a fence. You go across the street to get a better perspective—now look at the house with a proprietary feeling, a sense of being an owner. The house too has a hold on you.

I am not talking here about your right to sell or donate a property, nor am I talking about your possessions. I am concerned about this sense of ownership. Ownership is one of the biggest bluffs in the creation. It does not stand inquiry. Therefore, we need to understand that 'possession' is the reality whereas 'ownership' is *adhyāsa*. We must separate the two. We possess the house, but ownership is purely a projection. A flat in a high-riser in Bombay proves this point. The so-called 'owner' has really nothing there to own except his right to sell, or donate. He cannot demolish it or alter it drastically. What does he own?

In the Lord's creation, we only possess a few things, and use a lot of things freely. When you say, "I am the owner of this flat", you are declaring in the very same sentence, you are not the owner of other flats on the floor; you are not the owner of floors in the building; you are not the owner of buildings in the street; you are not the owner of streets in the locality; you are not the owner of localities in the city; you are not the owner of cities in the country; you are not the owner of the countries in the continent; you are not the owner of continents on the planet; you are not the owner of planets in the system; you are not the owner of systems in the galaxies, and so on. Then what do you own? Perhaps a two-bedroom flat, a speck in the cosmos! Even if you own the whole earth, you own only a speck in the cosmos.

What I do not own is infinitely vast and what I own is miserably small. This is enough to make me feel small. Once I feel small, in spite of all my ownership, I feel inadequate. Once I have inadequacy, I have all other problems resulting from it. Being inadequate I am insecure; being insecure I am frightened, anxious, apprehensive. Thus, all the problems can be traced to the sense of inadequacy, which itself can be traced to the sense of ownership.

Thus, one side of *adhyāsa* is ownership; the other side is inadequacy. Once I feel inadequate I have to prove to myself, 'I am adequate'. I spend my whole life proving to others, 'I am somebody'. Is that not true? I need to be reckoned and receive approbation. They have to applaud me; only then I feel that I am somebody.

We Indians have much more of this problem than the people in the West. We always worry about what others think of us. This is unfortunate. It is one thing to take into account or to deliberate upon the opinion of others, but it is quite another thing to worry about protecting one's image based on what others would say. People even get married, apprehensive of what others would say. Concern about what others would say is the problem of most human beings.

I am as good as what I think about myself. There is nothing more. I can go through a variety of experiences. They are as good as my interpretation of them. My interpretation is as good as my knowledge. If I am ignorant, my interpretations would be erroneous and my life becomes a pile of wasted experiences. I struggle to prove myself to be somebody in the eyes of others, inasmuch as I think I am nobody. The feeling, that I am of no consequence, results from the feeling that I am the owner of this much, thereby limiting myself. Therefore, the education in our scriptures is to look at the things as they are.

YOU ARE ENDOWED WITH THREE POWERS

Your physical body is something given to you, a set of senses is given to you. You find yourself endowed with a body, which has got the built-in capacity to grow, to become an adult. This is given to you. Memory is given to you. Further, as a person you are endowed with three powers; the power to know, the power to will and the power to do. You have the power to know, a power that includes the power to explore, to enquire and to remember. This is the *jñāna-śakti*. Then you have the power to desire, to will, and to create: this is called *icchā-śakti*. When you have the power to desire, you should also have the power and the skill to fulfil the desire. This is called *kriyā-śakti*, a power to do, to act. Every human being is given these three powers.

Icchā-śakti, a capacity to desire, is an endowment. It is a privilege available only to human beings. Unfortunately, today it has been misinterpreted to the extent that many contemporary Vedantins say, "You must be free of desires; desires cause problems." This is wrong. Such a notion only gives rise to complexes. Desires cause problems only when you deliver yourself into their hands, when you have no hold over them. What causes problems is your surrender of thinking. You should surrender your notions and not your thinking; it is the thinking that makes a person a human being.

Icchā-śakti includes emotions also. There is sympathy, compassion, sharing, friendship and their opposites. They are your privileges; do not use adjectives such as 'negative' for them. I often hear this, even from some serious people, "Swamiji, I have got too many negative tendencies, and I have to uproot all these negative tendencies." This is a new complex, because you studied modern Vedanta. There are only tendencies, not 'negative' tendencies. Some of them are useful and some not so. Our *śāstra* does not use the word 'negative'. They recognise the problems and say you can be without them, for which you have to educate yourself. *Icchā-śakti* also includes anger, hatred, anxiety; these are natural but not healthy.

In order to fulfil a desire, you require both *jñāna-śakti* and *kriyā-śakti.* Every desire is backed by knowledge. You cannot desire what you do not know. Again, fulfilment of a desire calls for skills, resources and so on, which is *kriyā-śakti.*

EVERYTHING IS NATURAL

People divide the world into natural and unnatural; but there is nothing unnatural in the world. Some of the natural things are good for you; some of the things may not be good for you. There are a lot of people allergic to pollen, which is natural. In spring when the flowers blossom everywhere and everyone is out enjoying, one person remains indoors. He sees the flowers only through glass panes, because he is allergic to pollen. Therefore, this division of natural and unnatural creates fads in people. There are people who eat sprouts and greens, in the morning, evening, and all their life, so that they may live a few years more. I cannot understand their reason; perhaps it is to eat more sprouts in the time gained. In New York City, there is a doctor, who runs twenty-two miles a day, so that he can stay healthy and live a few years more. If you add up all the hours that he spends running in the street, it would be much more than these extra years that he might gain. This is what is called faddism.

CULTURE HAS A VISION

Crying is natural. In India, when death occurs, whether the bereaved wants to cry or not, the relatives will come and cry and make the bereaved also cry for ten days. They just cry it out, until there are no more tears to shed. In some cultures it is different. When death occurs people come, you receive them, and hold yourself in spite of all the grief. After ten days the poignancy of the whole thing comes back to you and hits you forever. You cannot get out of it.

We do not bury anybody. This is another beautiful thing about Hindus. If you keep on burying, the rate at which the population is growing, the whole mother earth will become a burial ground. When someone dies you cremate the body and see the ashes in your hands. That is the reality. That is the Vedic culture. It is healthy to cremate. We retain the memory by offering oblations to our ancestors for three generations. The person is gone but his memory remains in the heart. There is no *adhyāsa* here. My body is the proof that my father lived once upon a time. I know that the person is gone; but he is not gone, because I am here. He is retained in my heart. That is pragmatism; it is not *adhyāsa*. It is amazing how we look upon death itself. The more I see other cultures, the more I appreciate what is here. When one is dying, they bring the dying person from inside the house to the area between the first door and the second door. He is not brought out into the street because he is still alive, but he is not inside because he is dying. We prepare ourselves. It is not lack of love or attention; it is preparation. People begin chanting Lord's name and if the person survives he is taken inside again. There is no problem. That is pragmatism. Even when a *sādhu* is dying, he sits, closes his eyes and perhaps he departs. This is how we face the death. Death is not a problem for us. We are prepared for it, because it is bound to come, but not without a fight, a fight to live.

YOU DO NOT OWN ANYTHING

The physical body is complete, a marvellous piece of creation given to me, although I do not own it. Many others can make a claim on my body. The mother can say, "I bore this body. It is flesh of my flesh. It is mine, not separate from me." "No," says the father. "I am the *nimitta-kāraṇa*, the instrumental cause of this body. I was involved in its creation. It was I who provided the food necessary for this body to grow and the clothes and shelter to protect it." The society can also say it has a claim over my body. Collectively the efforts of many provided the things necessary for this body to be alive and healthy. The wife can say, "This body belongs to me after the marriage sacrament. I too have a claim." A child born to the marriage also will assert a claim, "This body has duty towards me, for me to stay alive and grow."

The claimants are countless: the family, the employer, the state; water, space, fire, air; goats, cows, sheep; worms, mosquitoes, bugs, ants, bacteria; grains, grass, fruits and vegetables. The vulture says, "Some day that body is going to be my dinner." "Oh, no," says the amoeba, "for generations it has been my home."

The more I understand the connections, I realise that I can only be a managing trustee of this body. I am the in-dweller of this body. It is in my possession. As a possessor I can say, 'my body' only in terms of possession, but definitely not in terms of ownership. Even the laws of the State recognise that bodies are entrusted. State laws prohibit suicide, since they recognise that the person only holds a body in trust. He has the right to maintain and not to destroy it. He has a possessive right only to make use of it.

Just as the body is given, so is a wife is given; a husband is given. The wife is not a property to be owned and dismissed; she is equal to the husband.

A husband is generally older, and since we respect age, the husband is respected. However, that does not make the wife inferior. It is not part of our culture. In marriage one is given to the other. She is a partner, and so is he. According to our *śāstra*, there is some connection between the couple. It is not mere coincidence. Otherwise among millions, why only this person should be my husband or my wife? There is a meaning, which I have to discover.

A child is given, even if it is from a test tube. It is also natural. It is possible, and you accomplish always the possible. Others who are my contemporaries, living beings, they are all given. Every plant, every tree, every animal, every bug, all of them are given to you; and you are given some more powers to create some of them. The forces, weak or strong, all of them are given. The whole universe is given. It is a fact. When it is given, definitely, you have to be objective; you have to appreciate the given. With this appreciation, you come to understand that there is a Giver.

CREATION IS SOMETHING INTELLIGENTLY
PUT TOGETHER

I find this world is a set up, intelligently put together. What is intelligently put together is a product, a creation. Intelligently means meaningfully put together. A cell is put together intelligently. Look at an orange seed. The orange seed does not look like an orange, much less taste like one and it is not even round. If you open the seed you do not see anything except the pulp. But this seed brings out the orange tree. In that orange seed there is everything to produce an orange tree. It produces only an orange tree and not a mango tree.

A multi cellular organism, like the human body, is very complex. We do not see all the complexity in the formative stage, but the genetic codes are there in the genes. It is like a memory bank with all necessary information as to what has to happen, how the cell has to divide itself, how the liver cells, brain cells and so on, are to be created. It is not an ordinary thing. There is so much knowledge. This physical body is a creation, a marvellous creation. It is intelligently put together. You look at any part of the body, and you will be convinced of this fact. These arms have the right number of joints; otherwise they would not be able to perform the functions they perform now. Eyes, ears, heart, legs, all these are not ordinary designs. The liver is a complex chemical factory that you cannot reproduce. The kidneys are the greatest filters ever created, while the heart is an amazing pump. Look at the function of the heart. It is a simple pump that continuously performs its function for a number of years. It takes a great deal of engineering and a lot of money to make an artificial heart. Again, the different parts of the body are exactly where they should be. The eyes are exactly where they should be and so are the ears, nose, tongue, the stomach and all the others.

When I move my arms and legs, the motion implies that there are physical laws involved, energy involved, remote control involved. Numerous muscles are worked for this purpose. We appreciate them only when somebody has a paralysis. The sense of smell, or the sense of taste is all put together. You cannot produce an artificial tongue. If you can, even then it is not artificial; you produce only what is possible. There are taste buds, for various tastes. We cannot imitate them. If you are a dispassionate thinker, you know that to produce an artificial thing you require knowledge. Just to produce a cell, people are breaking their heads. Generations of scientists have been working on it. Even today it is not wholly successful. If we do become successful in producing a cell, it will still be an amazing creation because it is put together. I consider it a creation when it is intelligently put together. A flower, a plant, is intelligently put together. In the plant there is physiology, biology, chemistry and so on. There is a reason why it should produce that chlorophyll, how it is able to photosynthesise. It is all knowledge; whether the plant has it or not, there is knowledge involved.

I find that everything is a marvel when I look into it. Every cell is a marvel. Even the man-made things such as rockets, computers and so on are all marvels. What is a greater marvel is that I have been given an intellect to discover and enjoy the marvels.

BODY IS A PART OF CREATION

I am given a physical body, a set of senses and a mind, and *jñāna*, *icchā* and *kriyā śakti*s in this body-mind-sense complex. Further, there is a scheme of things in which I stand, live, and breath life, a scheme called the world, which again, is given. To this world, I am immediately connected; I am a part of it. The world does not begin where my nose ends, but it includes me. This body-mind-sense complex is a part and parcel of the world. To think that this body is separate from the world is, again, *adhyāsa*, projection.

I have a special relationship with this physical body, a relationship that others do not have.

I can say 'it is my body,' inasmuch as I am the managing trustee of this body, others are not. Thus, in a sense, this body belongs to me. There is an intimacy between 'I' and this physical body, which is denied to others. Even an ophthalmologist must consult me before changing my glasses. He depends entirely upon me, to find out whether I see or not. Only I know what I see, and what I do not see.

NOTHING IS CREATED BY ME

Even when I create something by my own efforts and skills, I cannot claim to be the sole author of the product. I cannot say, 'This house is created by me.' I did not create the land on which my house stands. I did not produce the materials, which went into the making of the house. There were masons, carpenters, electricians, and plumbers; I authored none of them. I did not create the laws because of which the house is standing. In truth, I cannot claim the sole authorship over anything, and unless I have sole authorship, I cannot have sole ownership. Ownership, therefore, is only a projection.

Further, I did not create knowledge. Nobody creates knowledge. Newton did not create the law of gravitation; he only discovered it. He understood some of the laws that operate in the world, just as I understand what is here. I can put things together only when there is the possibility. I have to understand this, for which I require a faculty of understanding, which, again, is given. Whatever knowledge I have is received from a number of people. A number of persons have worked before me even when I discover something new. The discovery stands on the piled up knowledge of generations, like a scientist standing on the shoulders of the previous scientists. Thereby, he has a better view of things. To think, therefore, that I have invented something is wrong. You are sitting upon the hard work of so many minds, the entire humanity, from the Stone Age and beyond. If Darwin's theory of evolution is any clue, even the monkeys have worked to make this invention possible. Therefore, to say that is 'my' invention is nothing but *adhyāsa*.

Knowledge is not created because if knowledge is created, then it has to be created upon the ignorant mind. The ignorance in the mind would continue to exist even as knowledge takes place. It would form the firm foundation for the knowledge to stand on. But we do know that in the wake of knowledge, ignorance goes. Knowledge, then, cannot be created. It always exists; you only remove ignorance. You cannot even say, "I am the one who has removed the ignorance," because to claim that you require a means of knowledge, which also is given.

This world, which includes my body, is given. If I continue to be objective, I have to find out the Giver. I see the creation but do not see the creator, the Giver, and the one who started it; the one who maintains it. There is a doubt whether there is a Giver. If there is one, who is that one? This question will haunt every human intellect. Even a child keeps on asking, 'How come? How come? The question of the Giver, therefore, resolves only in the appreciation of the Giver.

All that is here is either known or unknown. Together they form the meaning of the word *sarva*, all. This 'all' is put together and, therefore, it is a creation. The putting together implies knowledge, and the knowledge does not rest on an inert substance. It must rest on a conscious person. If I look upon that being as the Giver, God, Īśvara, then I have a question. Where is He? This is an important question, a question that has to be answered.

Many theologies declare that God is not anywhere here. When one looks around, one does not find God. Therefore, they place God in a distant place from where He watches you. He can get angry. He punishes those who commit mistakes. He is, no doubt, all compassion but He will punish you. He is all mercy, but you must seek His mercy. I can understand if you have difficulty in accepting this God. An ordinary mortal in a powerful position would want you to ask for mercy, due to pride and sense of power. Do you say that God is no different? To think that God is someone who is there to punish people is blasphemy. He may have some laws: for an action, there is a reaction, which is His law. I can accept that. But to say, 'God in heaven is prying into your private affairs, so that He can pass judgement on you later,' is irrational. We have to analyse the location of the Giver and assimilate what Vedanta says on this.

UNDERSTANDING THE GIVER

The world is intelligently put together, serving a definite purpose, and therefore it is a creation, an intelligent creation, which implies knowledge and design on the part of the creator. In creating anything, the maker of a given thing must have the knowledge of that thing. Whether it is a pot, a shirt or sugar, you must know all about it before you can make it. The logic is: *yo yat-kartā sa tat-jñaḥ*, the creator of a given thing should have the knowledge of that thing. The creator of a pot has the knowledge of the pot.

When we extend this logic to the creation of the universe, it can be said that *sarvasya kartā sarvajñaḥ*, the creator of everything must have the knowledge of everything; he must be *sarvajñaḥ*, omniscient. Over and above the knowledge, the creator must have also the skill and power to create. So, the creator of the universe must have all the power and skill to create everything. In other words, the creator must be omnipotent, *sarva-śaktimān*.

Further, all knowledge and skill must rest in a conscious being. Therefore, the creator of the universe must be a conscious being, an omniscient, omnipotent conscious being. The appreciation of a creator as Īśvara is not a belief; it is part of growing up. It is a mature way of looking at things. You do not just take things for granted. Since an intellect is given to you, it is only proper to appreciate the being, the creator of this universe.

WHERE IS GOD?

That the creator is not anywhere around here seems to be quite clear to us. We, therefore, assign a place to Him that is beyond our reach, to which our sense perception, inference, and presumption have no access. We call that place heaven. Some people call it *vaikuṇṭha,* and some call it *kailāsa.* Let us call it heaven. Most of the people who believe in God, accept that He is in heaven. That there is a heaven is purely a belief. One can have that belief, but to conclude that God is in the heaven is illogical. Let us see how. If God in heaven created this world, then who created the heaven? Since heaven is also a part of creation, it would not have been there before creation. So, we have to say God created the heaven. The next question is: Where was God before the creation of heaven? The only place that is left is hell, which amounts to saying that God in hell created the heaven.

This is absurd. Who then created hell? God. Where was He before He created the hell? No answer. The absurdity of all this is very clear.

It is wrong to believe that God in heaven created the world. It is another *adhyāsa*, a superimposition on God. Recognising the absurdity of this concept is emotional maturity. Emotional growth is not possible unless one grows cognitively and gains certain stability in that understanding, so that the understanding is neither shaken nor negated later. Knowledge means that which is not subject to negation, *abādhitaṁ jñānam.*

THE MAKER AND THE MATERIAL ARE ONE

The question of God's location arises from the conclusion that He is not here, which as yet we have to prove. Again, we cannot get the right answers for wrong questions because the answer we get is in keeping with the question. If we ask the right question there can be a right answer. The question of God's location cannot be answered unless we look at the whole thing as our *śāstra*s do. When we inquire into the nature of the cause of creation, we find that there must be two causes for any creation: the maker and the material. The maker, the one who is responsible for creation, is called efficient cause, *nimitta-kāraṇa*. There must be some material out of which any given thing can be created. For example, for the creation of a pot, there must be a pot maker, the efficient cause, and some material such as clay or copper, out of which the pot is to be made. For baking bread, there must be a baker as well as the flour to make the bread. With reference to the creation of the universe, if Īśvara, God is the maker, the efficient cause, the question is: What is the material out of which God created this world? While inquiring into the nature of the cause of the creation, we must take into account the material cause also.

Where did the Lord find the material to create this universe? Here, we must also bear in mind that both space and time are part of the creation. Hence, before the creation, there is nothing outside the creation because 'outside' is a concept in space, which is not yet created. Therefore, there is nothing outside the Lord before creation. If that is so, then the material should be within the Lord, which is why He is called the Lord. Thus, not only is the Lord the maker, but He is also the material.

While explaining how the maker and the material of the universe are one, the Vedas give us the illustration of a spider. '*Yathorṇanābhiḥ sṛjate gṛhṇate ca,* just as a spider creates thread and withdraws it'[4] and so does the Lord create and withdraw the creation. The spider is the efficient cause of the web because it has the intelligence and the skill to create the web. We can infer its intelligence from the way it chooses the right place for the web where it would not be swept away by the lady of the house and where it can get its prey. The material for the web is the secretion of a gland, which is within the insect. Similarly, the Lord projects the creation and withdraws into Himself at the time of dissolution.

Dream is more an appropriate model to explain that the Lord is both the maker and the material of the creation. In dream you create the world merely by *sankalpa,* thought. You think of a mountain, the mountain is. Think of stars, the stars are. You think of a brook and the brook flows. You have prior knowledge of what you create in dream because you cannot dream of something that is totally unknown to you. If you should see a man with horns in a dream, you know both the man and the horns; somehow they get mixed up and you have a man with horns.

---

[4] *Muṇḍakopaniṣad 1.1.7*

Where do you go for the material of the dream objects? You are the material. Your memory is the material. Hence you are both the maker and material for the dream creation. You create wondrous mountains and the sky and the stars. There are many people standing on the earth, looking at the stars and wondering as to who has created their wonderful world. Some of them praise the creation, some of them write poetry, while all the time you are the maker, Īśvara of the creation. No one in your dream world knows who you are. Thus, the dream is an experiential model showing clearly that you are both the maker and the material.

Now, what was there before the dream creation? You cannot say there was nothing, that there was non-existence before the creation of the dream. You, the conscious person were very much there. You were sleeping before the dream. From sleep you enter the dream, a half-awake state, but you are awake to your memories. It implies that you were there before the dream. True, there was neither time nor space nor object nor situation before the creation of the dream world because none of these existed in sleep, although you were very much there. The self was there before the creation.

Similarly, for this empirical world, the Lord is both the creator and the material. This is the right vision of God, the Lord, a vision that is unfolded by the Hindu scriptures, the Vedas.

I call the Vedas, Hindu scriptures even though the word Hindu has come about in a peculiar way. It appears that somebody could not properly pronounce the word Sindhu; therefore he called it Hindu. You are called Hindu because somebody else cannot pronounce you. But Sanskrit is such a profound language that even for this mispronounced word it has a meaning: *him apaśabdaṁ duṣayati iti hinduḥ.* A Hindu is one who condemns falsehood, who goes after truth. For him life itself is a journey for the discovery of truth. Therefore, Hindu means the one who lives a committed life to discover the truth. Thus, the Hindu scriptures have this unique truth, which is either not found anywhere else or if found, it is not methodically unfolded.

GOD MUST BE UNDERSTOOD

This is not a religion which says that God is sitting somewhere and made this world, that He is the only God. Literally taken, they do not make sense.

There may be mystic expressions, the meaning of which we need to discover.

The Lord is both the maker and the material; this alone is logical. Any other concept of God is illogical, a concept to be thrown out of the window of your mind. A created thing cannot have an existence independent of the material. Creation can be independent of the maker, but not of the material. The shirt you wear is not independent of the fabric from which it is made. You cannot imagine a shirt independent of fabric, or some material even if you are a very imaginative person. It means that the shirt, the creation, has no existence independent of the material. There is no creation without material. Where the product, creation is, there the material must be. The product need not be where the material is, but the material must be where the product is. A creation can never be separate from its material cause.

The Lord can exist without being the world, but the world cannot exist without being the Lord. Where the world is, the Lord, the material cause must be. Therefore, space is the Lord and time is the Lord, which is why Hindus even worship time and space. We worship Lord Yama, the Lord of time, and the Lord of death. We worship space also. There is a temple dedicated to Lord Naṭarājā in Chidambaram, in the south of India. In that temple, we have what they call the *cidambara-rahasya,* meaning the secret of *cidambara. Cit* means the all knowing God and *ambara* means space. In this temple they worship the Lord as space. As a young boy, when I first went to this temple, I was eager to know about this *rahasya,* the secret. When the priest removed the curtain at the time of *ārati,* I found there was no form. All that was there was a garland of golden *bilva* leaves hanging in space. It took years for me to understand this *rahasya,* secret. Similarly, there is a temple where air is worshipped as the Lord. In another temple fire is the Lord and so on. Only a *vaidika* can worship the elements, viz., space, air, fire, water and earth as the Lord. This is the vision of the Vedas.

The Lord is called 'he' from the standpoint of the maker and 'she' from the standpoint of the material. In fact, we use he and she interchangeably and use 'it' to indicate the truth of both of them. Since the Lord is everything, he is all the names, all the forms. We can, therefore, invoke him in any name, any form. This is a mature way of looking at the worship of God. Therefore, I can appreciate that one can worship him by kneeling, by lying flat, by a fire ritual, by elaborate *pūjās*, singing his praise, dancing, by performing one's duties, and in hundred different ways. We can pray to him in any language because he is omniscient and therefore knows all the languages. In fact, he should respond even before we call him. But we have to call him, invoke him, to make the worship real. A physical form of devotion is a necessity, because it converts a passing fancy of devotion into an abiding flame. All forms of worship are only to make one's devotion physical.

EVERYTHING IS SACRED

Ours is a religious culture. Religion is always involved in the life of a Hindu. We do not make divisions like secular and sacred. Everything is sacred for us because everything is Īśvara. The knowledge, in our culture, is classified according to the subject it deals with and not as secular and sacred, because all knowledge is sacred for us. Goddess Sarasvatī is the presiding deity of knowledge. On *Sarasvatī-pūjā* day, we make a pile of our books— *Gītā*, *Rāmāyaṇa*, *Mahābhārata*, Indian History and all the rest—to make an altar for the Goddess, and we offer prayers. A book is a symbol of knowledge;

a symbol of Goddess Sarasvatī and therefore, no Hindu will consciously step on a book. By chance, if you step on a book, you seek pardon - it does not matter what the book is about. Any book is a symbol of knowledge and therefore sacred.

Money is also sacred in our culture because it is a symbol of Goddess Lakṣmī, so we never deliberately step on a currency note. Lakṣmī stands not only for wealth but also for all other resources—skill, time, manpower and so on. Even the partner in one's life and the domestic happiness is looked upon as Lakṣmī; hence we look upon them as sacred. There is nothing secular or profane in the world. Everything is sacred and profound, because everything is Īśvara. The Indian religious culture is based on this vision. In terms of living rightly, this is the last word in human thinking.

There is nothing inert in the world, because the Lord is both the maker and the material. Just as your nose is inert but is still a part of you, the conscious being, similarly the creation is the extension of Īśvara. Hence there is nothing inert in the creation. Thus, space is the Lord, air is the Lord, fire is the Lord, water is the Lord, earth is the Lord, and the food in your plate is the Lord. The *prāṇa* inside this body, which digests the food, is also the Lord. Lord Kṛṣṇa says in the *Bhagavad Gītā* that He is the food that we eat, He is the digestive power in the stomach, and He is also the eater. As for the senses, they are also Bhagavān, the Lord; the mind is Bhagavān; the intellect is Bhagavān and behind all this is the *caitanya*, awareness. All these are Bhagavān. This recognition is called surrender. If all that is there is only the Lord, then you can either say, 'Lord is everything' or 'I am everything.' Both are one and the same. If everything is the Lord then what is mine? There is nothing that I can claim as mine; the concept of ownership is a projection, *adhyāsa*.

You can surrender your notions

People say, 'I surrender everything to you, Lord'. But everything already belongs to the Lord; nothing belongs to you. Then what do you surrender? Out of sheer ignorance you have misappropriated what belongs to the Lord and call it 'mine.' You can surrender only the *adhyāsa*, this notion. When that notion is surrendered you find the whole world becomes sacred.

The *Īśāvāsyopaniṣad* says, '*īśā vāsyam idaṁ sarvam*, everything is to be envisioned as the Lord'. All these belong to Īśvara and are non-separate from Him. Therefore, to say that I am inferior or that I am useless is *adhyāsa*.

Everything is a blessing. Your body, your mind, your senses, all given to you. It is a blessing, and you deserve it. You cannot wait a day longer for this blessing. You are not inferior to anybody. You have powers, all given to you by Bhagavān. Enjoy those powers. You see how free you are. When you see that all that is there, including 'you' is Bhagavān, there is surrender. In that surrender, there is freedom. Surrender is freedom.

Oṁ Tat Sat

Books by Swami Dayananda Saraswati

Public Talk Series :

1. Living Intelligently
2. Need for Cognitive Change
3. Discovering Love
4. Successful Living
5. The Value of Values
6. Vedic View and Way of Life

Upaniṣad Series :

7. Muṇḍakopaniṣad
8. Kenopaniṣad

Moments with Oneself Series :

9. Freedom from Helplessness
10. Living versus Getting On
11. Insights
12. Action and Reaction
13. The Fundamental Problem
14. Problem is You, Solution is You
15. Purpose of Prayer
16. Vedanta 24x7
17. Freedom
18. Crisis Management
19. Surrender and Freedom
20. The Need for Personal Reorganisation
21. Freedom in Relationship
22. Stress-free Living

Text Translation Series :

23. Śrīmad Bhagavad Gītā
(Text with roman transliteration and English translation)

Stotra Series :

24. Dipārādhanā

25. Prayer Guide
(With explanations of several Mantras, Stotras, Kirtans and Religious Festivals)

Exploring Vedanta Series : (*vākyavicāra*)

26. śraddhā bhakti dhyāna yogād avaihi
ātmānaṁ ced vijānīyāt

Bhagavad Gītā Series :

27. Bhagavad Gītā Home Study Program
Vol 1-4 (Hardbound)

28. Bhagavad Gītā Home Study Program
Vol 1-4 (Softbound)

Essays :

29. Do all Religions have the same goal?

30. Conversion is Violence

31. Gurupūrṇimā

32. Dānam

33. Japa

34. Can We?

35. **Teaching Tradition of Advaita Vedanta**